Prepping Made Simple

The *Best* Field Manual for New Preppers in a Hurry.

Corey Pankhurst

Table of Contents

Dedication

This book is dedicated to my loving family. Without your support, none of the things I enjoy would be worth doing. Thank you sincerely for *always* loving me and supporting my ambitions, no matter how crazy they may be.

Introduction

When I first began to investigate what it meant to be a prepper, I was surprised at the rather massive amounts of passionate, well-intentioned people who were more than willing to offer their *own* definition about what exactly it meant to be a prepper. I say "their own definition" because it seemed like everyone defined what it meant to be a prepper uniquely, depending on their own preconceived ideas and thought processes.

Some people suggested that having a few cans of veggies stashed away was enough. Others suggested that in order to be a prepper, you must have lost your mind worrying about zombies coming to tear you limb from limb and armed yourself to the teeth to combat such an obvious threat. Unfortunately for me, there were so many unique and frankly, contradictory definitions, I quickly became lost and overwhelmed with my findings.

I was greeted by countless lists of "must haves" and cardinal rules you *must* follow to consider yourself a prepper. Finding little to no guidance on how to achieve those things, I felt less than encouraged from the lessons I was presented with on my quest for knowledge. So, left with more questions than answers, I set out on a mission to master this prepper mindset I had been chasing, and write my own rules for living a prepper lifestyle. I was hellbent on preparing for whatever unimaginable and gruesome challenges the world may throw at me, but where was I to begin this well-intended mission?

I began by making lists of all of the horrid things I had learned from the Prepper Gods on YouTube and the forums I had dove headfirst into during my research. I took inventory of things I already had at my disposal, and took notice of areas in which I was lacking. I quickly realized that many of the apocalyptic scenarios that these prepper folks had been describing, while possible, seemed less likely than more realistic, yet less exciting scenarios. So, I changed my course and set sail for more practical shores. Yes, my whole mindset changed once I came to the realization that many of the so-called experts were selling fear instead of actual, practical knowledge.

Nowadays, I spend my free time helping others to create plans to make their own prepping journey a success. I tend to lead toward more realistic problems they may face, while leaving cataclysmic disaster prepping as an end goal, and not a first step, much to the dismay of those same Prepper Gods I had idolized a few years ago.

Contained within this book are the blueprints for how to prepare for things both big and small. We will cover everything from financial preparation, food and water stockpiling, bugging in, bugging out, home defense, and how to take the first step toward a prepared lifestyle.

If you are looking for information about who to blame for the world ending and how you can *shoot* your way out of any apocalypse the world may create for you, I am afraid to tell you, you will not find those types of fairy tales here. This book is intended to be a tool to help you craft a plan to begin your journey with a level-head, and teach you realistic, practical prepping for the modern age.

Though the world is definitely getting scarier as time moves forward, regardless of your age, race, gender, income, or location, it is not too late to begin preparing for uncertain times. Together, we will take our first steps as preppers and change the way we think about what it means to be a prepper in this modern era.

As the introduction comes to a close, I challenge you to think about your loved ones. They are likely the reason you have decided to become a more prepared person, and they are likely the ones you are choosing to protect. Think about all the reasons you need to succeed, and the rest will come more easily. The road ahead is not an easily traveled one, but it is a necessary path toward preparedness.

Changing your mindset, adding the knowledge to create a practical survival plan, and giving you the understanding of what it truly means to be prepared will not only offer the building blocks required to take you from the starting line to the finish line, but will allow you to run the race with confidence.

"Being ignorant is not so much a shame as being unwilling to learn."
-Benjamin Franklin

The First Step

According to a poll conducted by Bankrate, 56% of Americans are unable to cover an unexpected $1,000 bill with their savings. What that means is, should those people encounter an unexpected $1,000 expense, the majority would have to take on debt either in the form of a personal loan, adding to existing credit card debt, or borrowing from family and friends.

Now, if 56% of Americans cannot foot a surprise $1,000 bill, how many people are prepared for job loss or an income reduction? Even a short term income reduction would put the majority of the population in a very difficult situation. Covid-19 affected everyone differently of course, but we all undoubtedly know at least one person whose income was either cut completely, or was at very least reduced due to the lock-down orders that forced us all to stay home in 2020.

We learned a good deal about what it looks like when everything comes to a screeching halt from the Covid-19 virus. So, what can we do to prepare for job loss or income reductions in the future?

For starters, I want to make it clear that we are not planning for an early retirement here. There are tons of books on that subject, written by people who are far more qualified than I am to offer financial advice. Instead, our goal is to build up enough cash reserves to be able to afford to live our lives should we encounter a job loss for 3-6 months or possibly longer.

Now, I know what you're thinking.. "How can I possibly just manifest *that* kind of money?"

The short answer is, you can't. You cannot just wish a pile of money into existence. If that were possible, we would all be able to rush out and purchase 30 years worth of preps before the end of the week and forget about it. However, with a look into your finances, it doesn't need to be a hugely daunting process, either.

First thing is first; it's time to make a budget. Now listen, I get it.. A budget is not fun, and a budget is not sexy, but a budget is a very valuable tool to get your finances under control. In order for your budget to be effective, you must be completely honest about everything you spend money on, and you must be diligent in your efforts to stick to your planned spending amounts. It may not seem like much, but that $3.00 coffee habit will really add up at the end of the month if you neglect to record your spending. If you have ever read Dave Ramsey's, Total Money Makeover, this thought process may sound familiar so far.

I want it on record that I am not one of those people who believe that "if millennials would just stop buying their avocado toast, they would be able to end their money woes once and for all.." but the fact remains that every dollar you can cut from your non life-sustaining expenses will impact how quickly you are able to save up money.

Once you have a budget in place and have faithfully recorded and accounted for exactly where all of your money is going from month to month, put a plan in place to save 10% of your total income. Keep it somewhere liquid, such as a savings account or second checking account for the time being. The reason you want to keep it liquid is *not* to tempt yourself, but to have easy access should an emergency present itself.

Your first financial milestone should be $1,000. $1,000 is a great place to start because it is a large enough number that it will likely take you a little time to achieve, but not so large that the process is impossible. If you find that your expenses outweigh your income, you need to get that issue sorted out quickly. Try to take on extra hours at work, or come up with a side hustle to make up the difference so that you have 10% of all income going into savings.

This process becomes infinitely easier if both you and your partner agree to participate in the savings. If only one of you is on board, your partner may not be comfortable with the idea of forgoing some of the creature comforts such as take out or daily coffee purchases that you have both been accustomed to, so I highly advise you sit down with your partner and have a serious discussion about why you want to start saving some money.

Once you have begun working toward your first goal, make a policy between you and your partner on what constitutes an "emergency" and what doesn't. For example, Christmas gift money and vacation do not count as an emergency. A flat tire that needs to be replaced to allow you or your partner to get to work does count as an emergency.

To help keep each other honest, make it a rule that before the money can be withdrawn from the account, you both must sit down together and have a vote on if it is necessary or not. What you consider an emergency and what your partner considers an emergency may be two very different things, so by having a money meeting, you take away any possible issues that may develop from it.

When your $1,000 milestone has been reached, double it to $2,000. Continue this pattern until you have saved up 6 months worth of expenses or whatever end-goal you and your partner agree to, according to your budget.

Emergencies may still arise (and they likely will) while you are in the process of building your major fund, so expect setbacks. If you should experience some sort of financial hardship and have to borrow against your emergency fund, pause your savings temporarily until the emergency has passed, and then build back up to your current milestone goal you were working on.

As an example, if you are closing in on your $1,000 goal and you need to replace the transmission in one of your vehicles, it will likely take the vast majority of your savings to replace. While it will likely seem extremely frustrating to have to be in a position to start your savings over again, your savings did exactly what it was intended to do.

In this scenario we just described, you were able to fix your broken vehicle without having to take on debt. Even if you have to start from essentially $0, it is vital that you rebuild your savings as quickly as you can if you intend to make any progress toward your goal of 6 months expenses stashed away.

The ultimate goal here is that you build up a sizable nest egg to provide protection against large emergencies, job loss, or income reduction. The more you have saved, the more protected you will be. In the event you or your partner do experience a large financial change, there are actions you should take immediately to stretch your money even further.

Take a look at your budget.. Anything that is categorized as "extra" or "miscellaneous" should immediately be paused in the event of a financial emergency. Any revolving bills that you can temporarily pause will lighten your financial obligations until your situation improves. Streaming services, gym memberships, book-of-the-month clubs, etc, all fit into the "pause it!" category.

Consider pausing or decreasing any retirement accounts you contribute to if the income reduction puts your expenses above your income levels as well. An extra 5%-10% savings from your contributions can go a long way if you find yourself in a bad situation!

Most self-proclaimed "Prepper Guru's" advise that your initial action should be to stockpile food, water, guns and ammunition. Trust me when I tell you, those things are important, and are in the book later on. I am here to tell you however that if you have 30 guns, but no food, your priorities are way off. If you have food, but can't afford your home to keep it in, your priorities are also way off.

The first step is to build up savings. Not gold and silver, and not stocks and bonds, but cash money that you can get ahold of in a short period of time. We are not trying to reinvent the wheel here, just saving for an extreme scenario that is far more likely than zombies or an alien invasion. I am by no means suggesting that prepping for cataclysmic events is a waste of time or resources, but the fact remains that those types of events, while possible, are statistically less likely to occur than job loss or income reduction in the immediate future.

While saving for unforeseen financial situations is the first step, that does not necessarily mean you must abstain from other preps, once you have strong savings habits established. Creating your budget, adding a 10% savings amount to your fixed monthly expenses, and keeping your nest egg liquid are all you really need for this first step to be successful.

It is absolutely possible and frankly, well advisable, to work on other steps of the process while still building your financial nest egg, though I would advise you to wait until you have a firm grasp on your budget and have proven to yourself that you are able to set aside your 10% savings amount faithfully.

If you should find that your 6 months amount is comfortable, consider raising the amount to 9 months or even 1 year. There truly is no limit to this step. 6 months is a great place to target when getting started, but the more you have put away, the better situation you will be in should job loss occur.

I want to close this step by letting you know that for the majority of people, this step will be one of the most difficult. If you have spent the majority of your life unconcerned with savings, feeling free to spend extra money on things you enjoy with little concern for the future, that can be a very hard habit to break.

I encourage you to do your best to follow this step as it is written, but modify it if absolutely necessary. The entire point is to reach the finish line, and while sooner is better, if you need to slow the growth in order to reach the goal, that is okay. If 10% is just too restrictive, try 8% or even 5%. Just make sure you are adding to your prepper account faithfull every month, and you will see growth.

"A smart couple with a healthy financial relationship is always talking about money and how they're handling it. If there's a medical emergency or a job loss, talk about it. If there's a windfall, talk about it. Your financial situation is a constantly changing thing."
-Michelle Singletary

The Second Step

Now that you have a firm grip on your finances, and dedicate 10% of all income to be put into a job loss fund, what is the second step? When most people think of "Prepping," this step is what comes to mind right away. The second step is food and water preparations.

FEMA (Federal Emergency Management Agency) recommends all households have 72 hours worth of food, water, and other emergency provisions per person living in the home in case of disaster. While I do not always agree with the government (in fact, I may be sick even saying I agree with the feds at all), I believe that a 72 hour kit is a perfect place to start!

72 hours worth of food and water is fairly easy to obtain, and comes with very little financial cost. Frankly, with a little planning, you can have this amount by the end of the week. To figure out exactly how much food and water you require to cover all members of the

household, first you must take an inventory of all members of the home itself.

As an example, if you are a family of four, you simply take the amount of food and water one person requires for 72 hours, (3 days) and multiply it by 4. This will tell you roughly how much food your family requires.

When building food preps, make sure the food you are stockpiling is food you and your family will actually eat. If your family unanimously hates rice, then it makes little sense to stockpile pounds and pounds of the stuff. Of course, if you are in a true survival situation, beggars can't be choosers. With that said, I would not put all my time and energy into foods that nobody wants when there are other options that will be more appetizing to the palates who will be consuming it.

Remember, you must assume that this food is for an emergency situation, so you must also assume there is a possibility you will not have a way to cook or cool the food or water. Therefore, the food you are preparing should be food that can be eaten as is, regardless of whether or not you have other options aside from conventional on-grid cooking and refrigerating measures.

For example, maybe you have a camping stove that you would like to use during a power outage. But, what happens if you experience a flood? Will your camping stove still work the same? Or what if you experience a blizzard and cannot use a campfire to warm meat? Backyard BBQ's require a fuel source, usually charcoal, propane, or wood. If the fuel is ruined or runs out, your BBQ is no longer useful for its intended purpose.

Instead, consider canned goods, or canned meats. Many of which are safe to eat straight from the can, and do not require additional cooking to become safe. In addition, canned foods and meats have a significant shelf life, therefore they do not require as close of attention to dates.

Of course, you can purchase premade 72 hour food kits which come in compact packaging, perfect for preppers who do not have a lot of extra storage space, such as those who live in apartments and mobile homes where storage space can be a rare commodity. These easy to stack food packs are ideal for elderly people as well as they tend to be lightweight, and do not require you to preserve the food yourself.

Once you have 72 hours worth of food, it is time to begin stocking water. The rule of thumb is that you should have 1 gallon of water per person, per day. This water will be used for cooking, drinking, as well as hygiene. So, using the same family of 4, you would need:

1 Gal x 4 People x 3 Days = 12 Gallons of Water

From our above formula, we can see that for our 72 hour kit, we would need 12 gallons of drinkable water for our family of 4. It is recommended that you rotate water every 6 months, and that water should be kept in a cool dark place until needed. A basement or closet makes a good place to store water. Adding 1-2 drops of unscented bleach per quart of water is a good way to disinfect and purify water for long term storage. Just remember to let it sit 2 hours after treating it before drink it to allow the bleach to mix and dissolve into the water completely.

In addition, the containers that the water is stored in should not be kept directly on concrete as the jugs can leech from the concrete, putting other elements into the water in the process. Also, do not store containers with other toxic chemicals, such as pesticides or gasoline as they can also leech into the water.

There are containers on the market that are better suited to hold your water than others.. They typically come in darker colors such as greens or blues to help keep any light out of your container, in turn decreasing the risk of mold and fungus. They are also of heavier gauge plastics, and must be made of food grade material.

Once you have your 72 hour kit of food and water established, begin expanding this amount. For example, 3 days worth of food and water is nearly half of a week's supply, so start working toward a week's supply next. Follow that up with a two week supply, and then one month. Of course, when you get higher in the duration of your food and water stockpile, the amount of time it takes to duplicate also increases.

What I mean is, while a 72 hour kit is a low, easily obtainable amount of food and water, a 1 year supply will likely take you months to obtain and stockpile. That is okay!

I recommend creating a spreadsheet with all foods, their locations in your pantry, and expiration dates for each item. Believe me when I say that this will be a time consuming project, but it will make keeping tabs on what you have, where it is, and when it expires so much more efficient in the long run. There is nothing worse than spending all of your time and energy building a long lasting food supply, only to discover that half of it is no good when you actually need to use it.

Now, earlier in this chapter, I said to stock foods you do not need to heat to eat, and I stand by that. With that said, now would be a good time to invest in items that will allow you to heat food to eat because eventually, cooking food will become a necessity, especially as your precooked food stockpile begins to dwindle.

I would strongly suggest you do not put all of your eggs in one basket. What I mean is, do not go all in on a propane camping stove, or all in on a wood burning stove, and do not go all in on a charcoal grill, etc. Instead, look to multiple options so that if one item does not work, you have other means to cook for your family. A way to boil water is also vital for water purification purposes.

The reason food and water comes in second after finances is that having money allows you to have and keep shelter, which is where you will be keeping your food and water. Having a year's worth of food is great, but if you lose your home because you have an extreme income reduction, it does you little good. Afterall, how much can you *really* fit in your car?

With that said, we told you in the first chapter that you can simultaneously work on a few of these steps at the same time. This is one of those times. I would absolutely not wait for you to have 6 months worth of expenses saved before you begin working on your food and water preps. In fact, once you have one month's worth of expenses set aside, I would immediately jump on a 72 hour kit, with the caveat being that you do not abandon step one in the process. Hunger and job loss often go hand in hand. Think about it, if you cannot pay your bills, you likely do not have extra money for food either. Be preemptive and begin stocking away food and water as soon as it makes sense to do so.

For tips and tricks to help you learn more about food and water preps, head over to www.facebook.com/startprepping where we post daily tips and tricks to help take your prepping to the next level.

Another way to help you acquire food is to take up gardening. Now I get it, not everyone has the time, energy, or space required to have a meaningfully sized garden. If you do however, you can give yourself a huge advantage in the way of food available to you and your family. Stocking long-term food is great, but it is hard to beat a fresh salad, especially when everyone else is stuck with rice and beans for every meal.

Planting a garden means you can have fresh, flavorful food options that are high in vitamins and minerals! It can be a real moral booster as well. In addition, having a garden is a good source of exercise to help you get/stay in shape for the potentially rough road ahead.

The Third Step

So far, we learned why having an income-reduction fund, as well as having a food and water stockpile are important. They both provide us with peace of mind for troubled times during realistic scenarios that may arise. The third step is all about continuing the learning trend we have been on in the last two chapters.

The third step is investing in yourself. That's right, investing in yourself is a very important step in the process. But, what does it mean to invest in yourself, exactly? Books, webinars, conventions, podcasts, forums and blogs, and of course video content such as YouTube are all great places to consume content to teach ourselves more about survival, food preservation, hunting and fishing skills, and bushcraft.

Personally, one of the very first topics I would research would be food preservation. Canning for example, can take months and months of practice to master, but having books to reference as you go through the process can greatly shorten that timeframe (as well as the cost associated with failed food preservation). Canning and food preservation books can be found everywhere online, or you can usually find them at yard sales! They may be well used if you choose to go this route, but the old books are often filled with notes from previous owners.

Pro Tip: Those notes left behind by previous owners can be a huge benefit as you are learning from other peoples trials and errors.

Another area to prioritize is the topic of health and safety. You can learn everything from herbal remedies for common ailments, how to give sutures to open wounds, how to splint a broken bone, and other things that may be beneficial to know in a scenario where you are unable to go to a hospital in case of an emergency. In fact, many companies offer CPR classes to their employees, especially if they are a first responder or a member of the company's safety committee.

Consider this third step as just as important as the first two steps. Knowledge, along with practice will be the thing that sets you apart from everyone else with a little bit of water and a little bit of food in an emergency situation.

This third step will likely take you a while to conquer because simply buying books is not enough. You need to also read them and understand them. I recommend purchasing printed books, whether they are paperback or hardcover, instead of eBooks whenever possible for one simple reason; if you lose electricity or internet, your ebooks are going to be much harder to access than a printed version will be.

Of course, you can purchase an eBook first if you want to read it at less of a cost before you purchase a printed version to make sure it is a resource you wish to add to your library, if you choose to do so. But the version you keep for later reference should ideally be of a printed variety.

Personally, this step is one of my favorites. I absolutely love watching my library grow. If you are not as much of a lover of books, this step may not be as fun for you. Personally, I still subscribe to the idea that knowledge is power, so for that reason I advise you to take this step seriously, and invest in your own knowledge and skill development early on in your prepping journey.

Put your newfound knowledge to the test, and build the skills you learn by using them in real life scenarios. Practice your bushcraft skills. Practice your suture skills. Practice canning and preserving food. Practice your medical skills. Practice, practice, practice, until you have these skills mastered.

Practice makes perfect, but practicing these skills becomes more fruitful when you have the knowledge to back it up, while also decreasing the amount of time it takes to master the skills you are trying to learn! Win-win!

Plus, you get a well stocked library to gloat about to other preppers in your circle. Who doesn't want to gloat from time to time? On a more serious note, a nice side-effect of being close with people who share your passion for preparedness is that you can loan and borrow books from other prepper libraries. In addition, you also can give and receive recommendations for forums, books, videos and podcasts with your survival community members.

The Fourth Step

In my opinion, the fourth step is one of the most *vital* to your success as a prepper. Some prominent people in the prepping community feel that what I am about to say is crazy, and that you should take a completely different approach, but I completely disagree with them in the majority of survival situations you may find yourself in should SHTF.

The fourth step is building a community of other preppers, however there is a catch to this. Your community needs to consist of fellow prepper minded people, but the people need to serve your cause in order to be worthy of your efforts.

For example, if you have a medical professional who is interested in prepping, they would potentially be a good candidate for your survival community because they have an expertise that would benefit you in a survival situation. If however, you have a buddy named

John who has absolutely zero interest in prepping but often says, "If SHTF, I am just going to come to your house," then John would not be a good fit for your prepping community. It is not because you do not love your friend John, it is because having a weak link in a prepping community can jeopardize all the other members, especially in an emergency situation.

There are a few different things to consider when you look for a community. For starters, I do not recommend going door to door to advertise that you are a prepper. I would not broadcast all the things you have accumulated, because that makes you an instant target for people should disaster strike. Instead, start with people you trust. Chances are, you have a pretty good idea of any friends or family members that may be interested in prepping. That is a good place to begin.

After vetting your friends and family members, consider networking at church or work. Of course, use some discretion so nobody thinks you are a domestic terrorist, but chances are, outside of your circle that is where most of adults you know will be hiding.

To start the conversation, you can simply ask them about how they feel about what is going on in the world. Ask them things to feel out whether they are preppers or not. From there, you can inquire about what they do for a living (skills checking) and do an assessment before you open the conversation more about your prepping experience and the possibility of joining forces and forming a community, or joining an existing community together.

A community is important, because it gives you the opportunity to compliment skills you lack from others in exchange for offering skills you excel at in return. It truly allows your team to succeed because you can, in a sense, recreate a small version of society where different people have different roles, and because of that, society works. The same is true for your community.

I strongly advise you to put as much effort into building a strong, tight knit community as you can. This can take years to come together and will mean that you need to be active in your local community. It will involve you training together, getting to know each other, and building plans together. The end results however will pay dividends in the way of shared workload, as well as comradery, and shared knowledge. Ensure you put in the work, and build a survival community.

One tough topic to contemplate is, what will you do when friends or family come knocking on your door in a SHTF scenario? If your cousin comes to your home with his family desperate for help, will you be able to turn them away? Consider that you have worked hard to prepare for disaster so that your family survives, and any resources you give away will quite literally be taking food out of your families stockpiles. Consider trying to introduce your family and friends to prepping now, before you are put into the terrible position of being forced to decide someone else's fate.

If they opt out of prepping for their own reasons, you and your community will need to agree on who is allowed in, and who is not after a survival situation has begun. Another approach to this very real problem would be creating small prep stockpiles for this very situation. I would highly recommend doing this after you have already created a sizeable stockpile for your own personal needs, but by creating a "to go bag" for people who are in need such as family and friends, you are able to help them, while also not inviting them into your home or inviting them to your private stockpile that was curated for your own family.

The Fifth Step

The fifth step is coming up with a way to defend all of the things you have worked so hard to acquire, as well as your family. While most people immediately think of guns, that does not necessarily need to be the case for every situation, and I'll explain a little bit later in this step.

Of course, owning guns has some pretty obvious advantages over knives, bow and arrows, and other, unconventional personal defense items. For starters, a gun allows you to "reach out and touch someone." Depending on what type of gun you use, you have the opportunity for quick follow up shots, should the initial one not neutralize the threat. Also, a gun, especially a smaller gun, like a pistol is easily concealable, allowing you to stay under the radar, to avoid unwanted attention from would-be threats.

Just like other tools, there is no "one size fits all" firearm option. You wouldn't use a pair of pliers to pound nails, right? Sure, in a pinch it will work, but it is less than ideal, and much less efficient than a hammer would be for pounding nails. The same is true for firearms. A pistol would probably be able to put meat on the table if you had no other option, but it is far less effective than a rifle or a shotgun. When it comes to home defense, your options vary, but you need to choose your best option for you and your family. Additionally, the firearm you chose for home defense will likely be different from your daily carry, and your daily carry will be different from your hunting weapon. Consider different possibilities and options when choosing the right tool for the task at hand.

After saying all that, the best defensive weapon is the one you have. If you need to stop an intruder, a knife is an effective weapon when compared to your fists. A bow can still be lethal at ranges up to 50 yards. A baseball bat or a frying pan can cause a would-be assailant to think twice before striking. Use the most practical weapon you have at your disposal in the situation.

"I come bearing an olive branch in one hand, and the freedom fighters gun in the other. Do not let the olive branch fall from my hand."
-Yasser Arafat

The moral of the story is, while I absolutely do not recommend getting caught up in all the hype of needing 1,000 different guns with 20,000 rounds of ammunition for each one, there is nothing wrong with having the right tool for the job. What is more important than having an excessive amount of firearms at your disposal is proper training and practice with your firearms. Range time is your friend here, and you should be completely proficient with each of your firearms, and the only way to achieve that is with practice!

As far as how much ammunition you should have stocked up should you decide to go the "gun route" depends a lot on your situation. Basically, you should stock what you would expect to need. I know that is a very vague statement, but it is the most honest one I can think of. If you have a firearm you plan to use for both home defense and hunting, you would be wise to stock more ammunition for that weapon than you would if you had two separate weapons for those purposes, assuming they are different calibers, of course.

Another point to consider is, how many different weapons do you have that share the same cartridge size? If you have multiple weapons sharing the same sized round, consider having more quantity (and variety) for those weapons, as they will be in higher demand based on your personal arsenal's unique weapon count. For example, an AR15 and a Mini 14 both use .223, so if you own both of those rifles, it would be wise to stock heavier .223 ammunition quantities.

There are a few things to consider when choosing a caliber size, and one of the more important things would be how common the cartridge is. One reason is, if you have a hard-to-find round size, it makes it much more difficult to stock up, which makes it hard to practice with your firearm. The other reason is, in a SHTF scenario, you are much more likely to find common ammunition while scavenging for other supplies.

Some of the most common ammunition varieties, in no particular order are, .22LR, 9mm, .223/5.56 NATO, .308 Winchester, and 12 gauge. Any or all of these options are going to be the cartridge sizes you will be most likely to find while on supply runs in the event of a SHTF scenario. Choosing a weapon in one of these calibers will ensure that ammunition is obtainable to you.

You may consider having some of these ammunition varieties despite not having any firearms that accept them, as just as people may leave the ammunition behind should they decide to bugout in times of trouble, they may also leave firearms behind as well. I am not at all suggesting you rob your neighbors. In a survival situation, you must do what is necessary to ensure yours and your families survival, and if the survival situation lasts for a while, that may include supplementing your food, water, medical, etc stocks with scavenged goods from abandoned homes and businesses.

The Sixth Step

In the previous chapter, we introduced a new term that we haven't used yet. That word was "bug out." To bug out means to evacuate. Bugging out should always be a last resort, but that doesn't mean it is not important to have a bug out plan in place, just in case evacuation becomes necessary. Ideally, when someone needs to bug out, they have pre-planned destination(s) in mind, along with pre-packed equipment ready to go at a moment's notice.

A bug out location should be somewhere reasonably distant, but not so distant that you and your family can not easily get to it in a scenario where travel becomes difficult. The idea is, if things are bad enough for you to leave the safety of your home, traveling 4 blocks away is unlikely to be of great enough distance to offer protection from the thing you are running from. Perhaps a small piece of land outside the city would be a suitable location? It is advisable that you have at least a small cache of supplies already on location in case you need to bug out, the location is already prepped for your arrival. In addition, it ideally would have access to tools and other things you may need, as it could very well be your home for a while.

As far as having supplies ready to go at a moment's notice, I am referring to a bug out bag. A bug out bag is typically a rucksack type bag containing food, water, emergency medical supplies, flashlights, and anything else an individual would need if they were to bug out, already put together into a convenient bag that you can grab and go with zero warning. A bug out bag is not to be confused with all life sustaining equipment to last you a year. A bug out bag is intended to get you from point A to point B, and typically has enough supplies for a few days.

Now, like I said earlier, bugging out should be an absolute last resort. The only reason someone would consider bugging out would be if they will place themselves in immediate danger by staying in their homes, such as a nuclear disaster knocking on their door, or an enemy invasion in your neighborhood that is going door to door looking for people. The advantage of bugging in is that you already have all of your preps stashed away, you have shelter, and you have your community to lean on in times of trouble. Even the act of bugging out itself is dangerous, as you are much more vulnerable to threats outside the safety of your four walls.

When bugging out, you lose home field advantage. You know your area's strengths and weaknesses, assuming you have done a thorough home security check. You know how long it takes you to get from one place to another, and you know what security your home has. You are aware of potential areas of attack to your home, based on difficulty and what direction attacks are most likely to come from. In addition, you have neighbors to watch your back, and have the opportunity to be notified of new news you may not be aware of.

We discussed community building in an early chapter. If you bugout, not only do you lose the community you worked so hard to build, but you now are a stranger in someone else's community. How trusting would you be if someone set up camp next door when disaster struck, and tried to join your community, reaping the benefits of your hard work? If you said, "not very," then you know how the people surrounding your bug out location would feel.

If you bug out, you are limited to the things you can fit in your vehicle, assuming you can even use your vehicle. You will be completely vulnerable once outside the safety of your home, and anything you cannot take with you is now able to be taken by scavengers as you are no longer able to defend it. Any garden you may have been diligently working on is now food for whoever finds it first, and you can assume that if the situation was bad enough for you to leave in the first place, your home will not be spared if it is known you are no longer living there. Expect it to be scavenged for supplies quickly upon your departure.

If you *must* bug out, have a plan in place, and practice getting to your predetermined bug out location multiple times. Have a working plan for who does what once you arrive so your location can be secured rapidly upon arrival.

For example, who is in charge of securing the location in the event an uninvited someone has already moved into the location? Who secures the water? Who unpacks the car? Who retrieves the caches you have stashed? Practicing this plan will ensure that in the unlikely scenario you must bug out, it goes off without a hitch.

It is recommended that you keep watch for a while after your arrival, to ensure no one watched you enter the property, especially people who see you as an easy target (think back to intruding into an existing community that you are not a part of).

Again, if your situation was bad enough to leave the safety of your home, it likely is bad for others as well, and if they did not prepare, they may be desperate for supplies.

If you have the option, bugging in is going to give you the greatest chance of survival 99% of the time. I cannot stress enough how times of survival are the worst times to try to look tough by dragging your family away from the safety and familiarity of your home. If you absolutely must bug out, I strongly urge you to have a plan in place, and follow it to the absolute best of your abilities to give you and your loved ones the best chance of survival.

The Seventh Step

The seventh step is something that may be overlooked by new preppers, but is still a vital step if you wish to be completely prepared for most common threats you may face. The seventh step is to plan for power outages.

You may notice I didn't say "rush out and buy a generator." While a generator is a great way to supplement your electricity demands short term, such as inclement weather causing a temporary power outage, thinking of "long term" options. Depending on where you live, you will have different electricity demands.

For example, if you live in the northern part of the country, you will need to heat your home for a few months of the year. In the south and the west, keeping cool may be more important to you. Both put large strains on a typical generator.

If you have a forced air furnace system, it does not matter how much electricity you have, if you do not have the fuel (lp, natural gas, fuel oil, or wood) you will not get heat from your furnace. As far as central A/C goes, it puts a huge strain on the electrical system, and the bigger unit you have, the more strain it adds. So, what to do?

For starters, heating can be accomplished reasonably easily with a woodburning stove. While a fireplace can heat a room, 80%-90% of the heat is lost up the chimney from an open fireplace. Alternatively, a closed wood burning stove loses an average of 20%-40% of the heat generated. In addition, a wood burning stove will radiate heat even after your fire has extinguished, as the steel the wood burning stove is made of will absorb heat.

A/C is a harder feat to overcome. Some preventative measures you can take would be to plant trees to cast shade on your house, cooling the internal temperature of the home. Canopy type trees can actually lower your electricity bill by around $10 per month. While $10 per month may not be a total game changer, it does translate to less demand on your generator in the event you experience a power outage.Also, you can overcome some effects of the summer heat by planning ahead when building/buying your home by being conscience of what direction your home is facing, window placement, etc.

There are a few different options if you opt for going off grid with your electricity. Basically, off grid means that you are disconnected from the power grid. The plus side is, no more electric bill. The downside however is the large upfront cost. For a whole-home solar electricity generation system, your upfront investment could be anywhere between $15,000-$30,000.

If you are lucky enough to live alongside a creek or river, and choose to use a micro hydro-electric system instead, expect to spend anywhere from $1,000-$3,000 per kW. In addition, the batteries used to store the harvested electricity must be replaced roughly every 15-30 years depending on brand, use, as well as other factors.

If you have a solar panel array in your backyard, especially if it is visible from the road, you have painted a target on your back. Think about it; if the power has been out for a week or more, people will be desperate for electricity. How long do phones stay charged, especially in an emergency situation when people are checking for updates, or trying to update concerned family members? Your solar panel array can become a telltale sign that you have electricity, heat/A/C, and possibly other things that desperate people may want or need.

Now, it may seem like I just gave you a lot of reasons to *not* invest in alternative energy. The benefits of having an alternative energy source, in my opinion, outweigh the costs. For starters, there are quite a few tax breaks to investing in alternative energy sources. Next up, pending an EMP, an act of god, or some other calamity, while the rest of the area is without power, you and your family will still have electricity.

In fact, in many places, you actually are able to sell excess electricity you can generate back to the power company in your area. Now, I should add that you do not get the same rates that they sell it for, but if you are able to produce an excess of electricity, you can make a little bit of money every month, so make sure you do your research on this part.

Of course, you cannot hide a solar array, and I already went into why having a solar array visible can be problematic. With that said, if you took the Fourth and Fifth Step seriously, this becomes less of an issue. If you created a community, then your community will not only already be aware of your off-grid electricity production, but they will also benefit from your electricity. Secondly, having a way to defend your home, your family, and of course your electricity generation system, your property becomes much more safe.

Desperate people are more willing to take risks than non-desperate people. With that said, just like electricity, people tend to take the path of least resistance. If it is widely known that your area is not friendly to looters and marauders, there is a good chance that they will move on to the next area where the threat is less problematic.

There is no guarantee that the threat will not attempt entry to gain access to your preps, but if there is a way to reduce the risk of an all out war in your front yard, I suggest you do your best to take actions to mitigate risks.

The Eighth Step

The eighth step is purposely put late in the list. I believe the eighth step is an important topic, but this step is more important in extreme situations, such as SHTF type scenarios than it is when preparing for smaller, more personal disasters.

The eighth step is all about barter prepping. For those who, like me, did not pay much attention in school, bartering is defined as the act of trading one good or service for another, without using a medium of exchange, such as money.

Bartering will likely not be much more common in the initial stages of emergency situations than it is now, pending some catastrophe, but once people realize that money no longer has any real value, it will become the new economy. Think about it; how many cash registers or POS do you know of that do not require either internet, electricity, or both? How many people do you know that carry more than $20 or $30 cash on a daily basis? Likely the answer is "not many." If the grid is down for more than a day or two and people are unable to purchase emergency supplies and food or fuel, panic will set in rapidly, and the unprepared will begin trading things as a way to acquire the things they need.

So, what type of items can you barter? Well, the short answer is that you can barter anything that is in demand. But if we were to try to narrow it down a bit, you may consider: food, water, batteries, ammunition, medical supplies including medication, drugs, alcohol, tobacco products, fuel, guns, knives, baby formula, diapers, and other similar items. By no means is that an exhaustive list, but these are some solid examples of a few different bartering items that are likely to be in higher demand.

There are a few different ways to go about this step. For one, you can of course stockpile some barter options, just like you did food and water. Plan ahead and stockpile items that have a long shelf life and that you expect to be in high demand in a SHTF scenario. You can brew your own alcohol. People will of course want good alcohol, but will become substantially less picky as time moves along. You can buy extra ammunition in common cartridge sizes with the sole purpose of bartering it. (think 9mm, .22LR, 12 Gauge, and 5.56 Nato, for example)

Having a mighty arsenal of barter items at the ready will allow you to trade for things you need in survival situations. Again, this will become more prominent if you are in a long-term situation, but if you find yourself in that scenario, you will be happy that you took the time to think ahead about potential barter items that may benefit you in the future.

Many of the Prepper Gods online suggest precious metals as barter items. While that may be a reasonable idea early on, I personally do not foresee precious metals such as gold and silver holding value in extreme SHTF scenarios. For those reasons, I would not hold a large amount of precious metals in my barter preps. Consider redistributing the money you would have spent on gold and silver into ammunition and surplus medical supplies.

Your survival community may have feelings that differ from my own on this unique point, and while it is important to get along well with your survival community, it is up to you to make this decision of holding precious metals for barter purposes for yourself.

The Final Step

You have almost done it. You have put in the work, and you have put in the time. You have taken a leap of faith, investing your efforts into securing a more prepared future for both you and your family. What is there left to do to complete your prepper journey?

All that remains is to put all you have learned into practice. Take all of the things you have learned, and ensure you are proficient in every step we have gone over. Practice at the shooting range. Keep your budget running and accurate. Have conversations with your partner about plans and "what if's." Make and practice home defense roles, and what to do in the event of an intruder. Continue stocking up (and reading) books pertinent to your knowledge shortcomings.

Truth be told, you will never be 100% completely prepared for *every* possible scenario that you may possibly encounter. Do not let that fact disappoint you. Instead, use it as fuel to push you to continue on your prepping journey. I firmly believe it is not too late to begin living a prepping lifestyle.

"It has been said that the best time to plant a tree was 30 years ago, the second best time is today."
-Chinese Proverb

Push yourself to be the provider and protector your family deserves by preparing for what they may not see coming today. It is your responsibility to care for and defend your family, after all.

I want it on record, this book is not an all-encompassing encyclopedia of prepping. It isn't intended to be a one-stop-shop and I do not wish to pretend that it is. What this book *does* however, is teach new, prepper-minded people how to get started on their journey, a journey that can save their lives.

I firmly believe that following the instructions in this book will give you the tools to be not only more prepared than when you started this book, but also a valuable community member, whether you join an existing survival community, or form your own. If you feel that this book has benefited you, or aided you in becoming a better prepper, I am honored to have played a small role in your development.

This is the point of the book where I offer you a sincere "Thank You" for taking the time to read this book. I hope it has served you well, and I hope it continues to serve you well as you begin your quest for a more prepared life. If you have found value in these pages, consider leaving a positive review wherever you purchased this book. It would be highly appreciated.

Until next time, happy prepping!